Student information

Name: _____

Allergies: _____

`I0387717`

Parent / Caregiver Name: _____
Mobile phone: _____
Home phone: _____
Work phone: _____
Email: _____

Parent / Caregiver Name: _____
Mobile phone: _____
Home phone: _____
Work phone: _____
Email: _____

Extra Information:

_____
_____
_____
_____
_____
_____

Monday   Week beginning: _____

My day was:

😀   🙂   😐   🙁   ☹️
fantastic   good   okay   not good   awful

Teacher:

Parent:

Tuesday

My day was:

😀   🙂   😐   🙁   ☹️
fantastic   good   okay   not good   awful

Teacher:

Parent:

Wednesday

My day was:

😀   🙂   😐   🙁   ☹️
fantastic   good   okay   not good   awful

Teacher:

Parent:

Thursday

My day was:

- 🙂 fantastic
- 🙂 good
- 😐 okay
- 🙁 not good
- ☹️ awful

Teacher:

Parent:

Friday

My day was:

- 🙂 fantastic
- 🙂 good
- 😐 okay
- 🙁 not good
- ☹️ awful

Teacher:

Parent:

Extra Space:

Monday   Week beginning: _____

My day was:

😀   🙂   😐   🙁   😧

fantastic   good   okay   not good   awful

Teacher:

Parent:

Tuesday

My day was:

😀   🙂   😐   🙁   😧

fantastic   good   okay   not good   awful

Teacher:

Parent:

Wednesday

My day was:

😀   🙂   😐   🙁   😧

fantastic   good   okay   not good   awful

Teacher:

Parent:

Thursday
My day was:

😃 fantastic   🙂 good   😐 okay   🙁 not good   ☹️ awful

Teacher:

Parent:

Friday
My day was:

😃 fantastic   🙂 good   😐 okay   🙁 not good   ☹️ awful

Teacher:

Parent:

Extra Space:

_____
_____
_____
_____
_____
_____
_____

Monday   Week beginning: _____

My day was:

   😀   🙂   😐   ☹️   😣

fantastic   good   okay   not good   awful

Teacher:

Parent:

Tuesday

My day was:

   😀   🙂   😐   ☹️   😣

fantastic   good   okay   not good   awful

Teacher:

Parent:

Wednesday

My day was:

   😀   🙂   😐   ☹️   😣

fantastic   good   okay   not good   awful

Teacher:

Parent:

Thursday

My day was:

| fantastic | good | okay | not good | awful |

Teacher:

Parent:

Friday

My day was:

| fantastic | good | okay | not good | awful |

Teacher:

Parent:

Extra Space:

Monday   Week beginning: _____

My day was:

fantastic   good   okay   not good   awful

Teacher:

Parent:

Tuesday

My day was:

fantastic   good   okay   not good   awful

Teacher:

Parent:

Wednesday

My day was:

fantastic   good   okay   not good   awful

Teacher:

Parent:

Thursday

My day was:

fantastic   good   okay   not good   awful

Teacher:

Parent:

Friday

My day was:

fantastic   good   okay   not good   awful

Teacher:

Parent:

Extra Space:

Monday   Week beginning: _____

My day was:

😄   🙂   😐   🙁   ☹️
fantastic   good   okay   not good   awful

┌───┐
│ Teacher: │
│   │
└───┘

┌───┐
│ Parent: │
│   │
└───┘

Tuesday

My day was:

😄   🙂   😐   🙁   ☹️
fantastic   good   okay   not good   awful

┌───┐
│ Teacher: │
│   │
└───┘

┌───┐
│ Parent: │
│   │
└───┘

Wednesday

My day was:

😄   🙂   😐   🙁   ☹️
fantastic   good   okay   not good   awful

┌───┐
│ Teacher: │
│   │
└───┘

┌───┐
│ Parent: │
│   │
└───┘

Thursday

My day was:

😊 fantastic   🙂 good   😐 okay   🙁 not good   ☹️ awful

Teacher:

Parent:

Friday

My day was:

😊 fantastic   🙂 good   😐 okay   🙁 not good   ☹️ awful

Teacher:

Parent:

Extra Space:

_____
_____
_____
_____
_____
_____

Monday Week beginning: _____

My day was:

fantastic   good   okay   not good   awful

Teacher:

Parent:

Tuesday

My day was:

fantastic   good   okay   not good   awful

Teacher:

Parent:

Wednesday

My day was:

fantastic   good   okay   not good   awful

Teacher:

Parent:

Thursday

My day was:

😊	🙂	😐	🙁	😧
fantastic	good	okay	not good	awful

Teacher:

Parent:

Friday

My day was:

😊	🙂	😐	🙁	😧
fantastic	good	okay	not good	awful

Teacher:

Parent:

Extra Space:

Monday   Week beginning: _____

My day was:

😀 fantastic   🙂 good   😐 okay   🙁 not good   ☹️ awful

```
┌─────────────────────────────────────────────┐
│ Teacher:                                    │
│                                             │
└─────────────────────────────────────────────┘
┌─────────────────────────────────────────────┐
│ Parent:                                     │
│                                             │
└─────────────────────────────────────────────┘
```

Tuesday

My day was:

😀 fantastic   🙂 good   😐 okay   🙁 not good   ☹️ awful

```
┌─────────────────────────────────────────────┐
│ Teacher:                                    │
│                                             │
└─────────────────────────────────────────────┘
┌─────────────────────────────────────────────┐
│ Parent:                                     │
│                                             │
└─────────────────────────────────────────────┘
```

Wednesday

My day was:

😀 fantastic   🙂 good   😐 okay   🙁 not good   ☹️ awful

```
┌─────────────────────────────────────────────┐
│ Teacher:                                    │
│                                             │
└─────────────────────────────────────────────┘
┌─────────────────────────────────────────────┐
│ Parent:                                     │
│                                             │
└─────────────────────────────────────────────┘
```

Thursday

My day was:

😃	🙂	😐	🙁	😟
fantastic	good	okay	not good	awful

Teacher:

Parent:

Friday

My day was:

😃	🙂	😐	🙁	😟
fantastic	good	okay	not good	awful

Teacher:

Parent:

Extra Space:

Monday   Week beginning: _____

My day was:

| fantastic | good | okay | not good | awful |

Teacher:

Parent:

Tuesday

My day was:

| fantastic | good | okay | not good | awful |

Teacher:

Parent:

Wednesday

My day was:

| fantastic | good | okay | not good | awful |

Teacher:

Parent:

Thursday

My day was:

| fantastic | good | okay | not good | awful |

Teacher:

Parent:

Friday

My day was:

| fantastic | good | okay | not good | awful |

Teacher:

Parent:

Extra Space:

Monday   Week beginning: _____

My day was:

fantastic   good   okay   not good   awful

Teacher:

Parent:

Tuesday

My day was:

fantastic   good   okay   not good   awful

Teacher:

Parent:

Wednesday

My day was:

fantastic   good   okay   not good   awful

Teacher:

Parent:

Thursday

My day was:

fantastic	good	okay	not good	awful

Teacher:

Parent:

Friday

My day was:

fantastic	good	okay	not good	awful

Teacher:

Parent:

Extra Space:

Monday   Week beginning: _____

My day was:

| fantastic | good | okay | not good | awful |

Teacher:

Parent:

Tuesday

My day was:

| fantastic | good | okay | not good | awful |

Teacher:

Parent:

Wednesday

My day was:

| fantastic | good | okay | not good | awful |

Teacher:

Parent:

Thursday

My day was:

- 😃 fantastic
- 🙂 good
- 😐 okay
- 🙁 not good
- ☹️ awful

Teacher:

Parent:

Friday

My day was:

- 😃 fantastic
- 🙂 good
- 😐 okay
- 🙁 not good
- ☹️ awful

Teacher:

Parent:

Extra Space:

Monday   Week beginning: _____

My day was:

😀 fantastic   🙂 good   😐 okay   🙁 not good   ☹ awful

Teacher:

Parent:

Tuesday

My day was:

😀 fantastic   🙂 good   😐 okay   🙁 not good   ☹ awful

Teacher:

Parent:

Wednesday

My day was:

😀 fantastic   🙂 good   😐 okay   🙁 not good   ☹ awful

Teacher:

Parent:

Thursday

My day was:

| fantastic | good | okay | not good | awful |

Teacher:

Parent:

Friday

My day was:

| fantastic | good | okay | not good | awful |

Teacher:

Parent:

Extra Space:

Monday　　　　　Week beginning: _____

My day was:

☺ fantastic　　☺ good　　😐 okay　　☹ not good　　☹ awful

Teacher:

Parent:

Tuesday

My day was:

☺ fantastic　　☺ good　　😐 okay　　☹ not good　　☹ awful

Teacher:

Parent:

Wednesday

My day was:

☺ fantastic　　☺ good　　😐 okay　　☹ not good　　☹ awful

Teacher:

Parent:

Thursday

My day was:

fantastic	good	okay	not good	awful

Teacher:

Parent:

Friday

My day was:

fantastic	good	okay	not good	awful

Teacher:

Parent:

Extra Space:

Monday

Week beginning: _____

My day was:

😀 fantastic   🙂 good   😐 okay   🙁 not good   ☹️ awful

Teacher:

Parent:

Tuesday

My day was:

😀 fantastic   🙂 good   😐 okay   🙁 not good   ☹️ awful

Teacher:

Parent:

Wednesday

My day was:

😀 fantastic   🙂 good   😐 okay   🙁 not good   ☹️ awful

Teacher:

Parent:

Thursday

My day was:

😊 fantastic   🙂 good   😐 okay   🙁 not good   ☹️ awful

Teacher:

Parent:

Friday

My day was:

😊 fantastic   🙂 good   😐 okay   🙁 not good   ☹️ awful

Teacher:

Parent:

Extra Space:

_____
_____
_____
_____
_____
_____
_____

Monday   Week beginning: _____

My day was:

fantastic   good   okay   not good   awful

Teacher:

Parent:

Tuesday

My day was:

fantastic   good   okay   not good   awful

Teacher:

Parent:

Wednesday

My day was:

fantastic   good   okay   not good   awful

Teacher:

Parent:

Thursday

My day was:

fantastic	good	okay	not good	awful

Teacher:

Parent:

Friday

My day was:

fantastic	good	okay	not good	awful

Teacher:

Parent:

Extra Space:

Monday   Week beginning: _____

My day was:

fantastic   good   okay   not good   awful

Teacher:

Parent:

Tuesday

My day was:

fantastic   good   okay   not good   awful

Teacher:

Parent:

Wednesday

My day was:

fantastic   good   okay   not good   awful

Teacher:

Parent:

Thursday

My day was:

😊	🙂	😐	🙁	😧
fantastic	good	okay	not good	awful

Teacher:

Parent:

Friday

My day was:

😊	🙂	😐	🙁	😧
fantastic	good	okay	not good	awful

Teacher:

Parent:

Extra Space:

Monday　　　Week beginning: _____

My day was:

☺ fantastic　　　☺ good　　　😐 okay　　　🙁 not good　　　😟 awful

Teacher:

Parent:

Tuesday

My day was:

☺ fantastic　　　☺ good　　　😐 okay　　　🙁 not good　　　😟 awful

Teacher:

Parent:

Wednesday

My day was:

☺ fantastic　　　☺ good　　　😐 okay　　　🙁 not good　　　😟 awful

Teacher:

Parent:

Thursday

My day was:

😊 fantastic   🙂 good   😐 okay   🙁 not good   ☹️ awful

Teacher:

Parent:

Friday

My day was:

😊 fantastic   🙂 good   😐 okay   🙁 not good   ☹️ awful

Teacher:

Parent:

Extra Space:

_____
_____
_____
_____
_____
_____
_____

Monday

Week beginning: _____

My day was:

| fantastic | good | okay | not good | awful |

Teacher:

Parent:

Tuesday

My day was:

| fantastic | good | okay | not good | awful |

Teacher:

Parent:

Wednesday

My day was:

| fantastic | good | okay | not good | awful |

Teacher:

Parent:

Thursday

My day was:

fantastic	good	okay	not good	awful

Teacher:

Parent:

Friday

My day was:

fantastic	good	okay	not good	awful

Teacher:

Parent:

Extra Space:

Monday Week beginning: _____

My day was:

😀 fantastic   🙂 good   😐 okay   🙁 not good   ☹️ awful

```
Teacher:

```

```
Parent:

```

Tuesday

My day was:

😀 fantastic   🙂 good   😐 okay   🙁 not good   ☹️ awful

```
Teacher:

```

```
Parent:

```

Wednesday

My day was:

😀 fantastic   🙂 good   😐 okay   🙁 not good   ☹️ awful

```
Teacher:

```

```
Parent:

```

Thursday

My day was:

fantastic	good	okay	not good	awful

Teacher:

Parent:

Friday

My day was:

fantastic	good	okay	not good	awful

Teacher:

Parent:

Extra Space:

Monday   Week beginning: _____

My day was:

| fantastic | good | okay | not good | awful |

Teacher:

Parent:

Tuesday

My day was:

| fantastic | good | okay | not good | awful |

Teacher:

Parent:

Wednesday

My day was:

| fantastic | good | okay | not good | awful |

Teacher:

Parent:

Thursday

My day was:

fantastic	good	okay	not good	awful

Teacher:

Parent:

Friday

My day was:

fantastic	good	okay	not good	awful

Teacher:

Parent:

Extra Space:

Monday　　　Week beginning: _____

My day was:

　fantastic　　good　　okay　　not good　　awful

```
Teacher:


```

```
Parent:


```

Tuesday

My day was:

　fantastic　　good　　okay　　not good　　awful

```
Teacher:


```

```
Parent:


```

Wednesday

My day was:

　fantastic　　good　　okay　　not good　　awful

```
Teacher:


```

```
Parent:


```

Thursday

My day was:

😃	🙂	😐	🙁	☹️
fantastic	good	okay	not good	awful

Teacher:

Parent:

Friday

My day was:

😃	🙂	😐	🙁	☹️
fantastic	good	okay	not good	awful

Teacher:

Parent:

Extra Space:

Monday   Week beginning: _____

My day was:

| fantastic | good | okay | not good | awful |

Teacher:

Parent:

Tuesday

My day was:

| fantastic | good | okay | not good | awful |

Teacher:

Parent:

Wednesday

My day was:

| fantastic | good | okay | not good | awful |

Teacher:

Parent:

Thursday

My day was:

😃 fantastic   🙂 good   😐 okay   🙁 not good   😣 awful

Teacher:

Parent:

Friday

My day was:

😃 fantastic   🙂 good   😐 okay   🙁 not good   😣 awful

Teacher:

Parent:

Extra Space:

_____
_____
_____
_____
_____
_____
_____

Monday   Week beginning: _____

My day was:

fantastic	good	okay	not good	awful

Teacher:

Parent:

Tuesday

My day was:

fantastic	good	okay	not good	awful

Teacher:

Parent:

Wednesday

My day was:

fantastic	good	okay	not good	awful

Teacher:

Parent:

Thursday

My day was:

| fantastic | good | okay | not good | awful |

Teacher:

Parent:

Friday

My day was:

| fantastic | good | okay | not good | awful |

Teacher:

Parent:

Extra Space:

Monday　　　　Week beginning: _____

My day was:

😃 fantastic   🙂 good   😐 okay   🙁 not good   ☹️ awful

```
┌─────────────────────────────────────────────┐
│ Teacher:                                    │
│                                             │
└─────────────────────────────────────────────┘
┌─────────────────────────────────────────────┐
│ Parent:                                     │
│                                             │
└─────────────────────────────────────────────┘
```

Tuesday

My day was:

😃 fantastic   🙂 good   😐 okay   🙁 not good   ☹️ awful

```
┌─────────────────────────────────────────────┐
│ Teacher:                                    │
│                                             │
└─────────────────────────────────────────────┘
┌─────────────────────────────────────────────┐
│ Parent:                                     │
│                                             │
└─────────────────────────────────────────────┘
```

Wednesday

My day was:

😃 fantastic   🙂 good   😐 okay   🙁 not good   ☹️ awful

```
┌─────────────────────────────────────────────┐
│ Teacher:                                    │
│                                             │
└─────────────────────────────────────────────┘
┌─────────────────────────────────────────────┐
│ Parent:                                     │
│                                             │
└─────────────────────────────────────────────┘
```

Thursday

My day was:

fantastic	good	okay	not good	awful

Teacher:

Parent:

Friday

My day was:

fantastic	good	okay	not good	awful

Teacher:

Parent:

Extra Space:

Monday   Week beginning: _____

My day was:

fantastic   good   okay   not good   awful

Teacher:

Parent:

Tuesday

My day was:

fantastic   good   okay   not good   awful

Teacher:

Parent:

Wednesday

My day was:

fantastic   good   okay   not good   awful

Teacher:

Parent:

Thursday

My day was:

| fantastic | good | okay | not good | awful |

Teacher:

Parent:

Friday

My day was:

| fantastic | good | okay | not good | awful |

Teacher:

Parent:

Extra Space:

Monday   Week beginning: _____

My day was:

fantastic   good   okay   not good   awful

Teacher:

Parent:

Tuesday

My day was:

fantastic   good   okay   not good   awful

Teacher:

Parent:

Wednesday

My day was:

fantastic   good   okay   not good   awful

Teacher:

Parent:

Thursday
My day was:

    fantastic   good   okay   not good   awful

Teacher:

Parent:

Friday
My day was:

    fantastic   good   okay   not good   awful

Teacher:

Parent:

Extra Space:

Monday Week beginning: _____
My day was:

😃 fantastic   🙂 good   😐 okay   🙁 not good   ☹️ awful

Teacher:

Parent:

Tuesday
My day was:

😃 fantastic   🙂 good   😐 okay   🙁 not good   ☹️ awful

Teacher:

Parent:

Wednesday
My day was:

😃 fantastic   🙂 good   😐 okay   🙁 not good   ☹️ awful

Teacher:

Parent:

Thursday

My day was:

| fantastic | good | okay | not good | awful |

Teacher:

Parent:

Friday

My day was:

| fantastic | good | okay | not good | awful |

Teacher:

Parent:

Extra Space:

_____
_____
_____
_____
_____
_____
_____

Week beginning: _____

Monday

My day was:

😀 fantastic   🙂 good   😐 okay   🙁 not good   😟 awful

Teacher:

Parent:

Tuesday

My day was:

😀 fantastic   🙂 good   😐 okay   🙁 not good   😟 awful

Teacher:

Parent:

Wednesday

My day was:

😀 fantastic   🙂 good   😐 okay   🙁 not good   😟 awful

Teacher:

Parent:

Thursday

My day was:

- 😊 fantastic
- 🙂 good
- 😐 okay
- 🙁 not good
- ☹️ awful

Teacher:

Parent:

Friday

My day was:

- 😊 fantastic
- 🙂 good
- 😐 okay
- 🙁 not good
- ☹️ awful

Teacher:

Parent:

Extra Space:

_____
_____
_____
_____
_____
_____
_____

Monday   Week beginning: _____

My day was:

fantastic   good   okay   not good   awful

Teacher:

Parent:

Tuesday

My day was:

fantastic   good   okay   not good   awful

Teacher:

Parent:

Wednesday

My day was:

fantastic   good   okay   not good   awful

Teacher:

Parent:

Thursday

My day was:

😀	🙂	😐	🙁	☹️
fantastic	good	okay	not good	awful

Teacher:

Parent:

Friday

My day was:

😀	🙂	😐	🙁	☹️
fantastic	good	okay	not good	awful

Teacher:

Parent:

Extra Space:

Monday   Week beginning: _____

My day was:

☺ fantastic   🙂 good   😐 okay   🙁 not good   ☹ awful

```
┌─────────────────────────────────────────────────┐
│ Teacher:                                        │
│                                                 │
└─────────────────────────────────────────────────┘
```

```
┌─────────────────────────────────────────────────┐
│ Parent:                                         │
│                                                 │
└─────────────────────────────────────────────────┘
```

Tuesday

My day was:

☺ fantastic   🙂 good   😐 okay   🙁 not good   ☹ awful

```
┌─────────────────────────────────────────────────┐
│ Teacher:                                        │
│                                                 │
└─────────────────────────────────────────────────┘
```

```
┌─────────────────────────────────────────────────┐
│ Parent:                                         │
│                                                 │
└─────────────────────────────────────────────────┘
```

Wednesday

My day was:

☺ fantastic   🙂 good   😐 okay   🙁 not good   ☹ awful

```
┌─────────────────────────────────────────────────┐
│ Teacher:                                        │
│                                                 │
└─────────────────────────────────────────────────┘
```

```
┌─────────────────────────────────────────────────┐
│ Parent:                                         │
│                                                 │
└─────────────────────────────────────────────────┘
```

Thursday

My day was:

- 😊 fantastic
- 🙂 good
- 😐 okay
- 🙁 not good
- 😞 awful

Teacher:

Parent:

Friday

My day was:

- 😊 fantastic
- 🙂 good
- 😐 okay
- 🙁 not good
- 😞 awful

Teacher:

Parent:

Extra Space:

Monday   Week beginning: _____

My day was:

😃   🙂   😐   🙁   😣
fantastic   good   okay   not good   awful

┌───┐
│ Teacher: │
│   │
└───┘

┌───┐
│ Parent: │
│   │
└───┘

Tuesday

My day was:

😃   🙂   😐   🙁   😣
fantastic   good   okay   not good   awful

┌───┐
│ Teacher: │
│   │
└───┘

┌───┐
│ Parent: │
│   │
└───┘

Wednesday

My day was:

😃   🙂   😐   🙁   😣
fantastic   good   okay   not good   awful

┌───┐
│ Teacher: │
│   │
└───┘

┌───┐
│ Parent: │
│   │
└───┘

Thursday

My day was:

- fantastic
- good
- okay
- not good
- awful

Teacher:

Parent:

Friday

My day was:

- fantastic
- good
- okay
- not good
- awful

Teacher:

Parent:

Extra Space:

Monday   Week beginning: _____

My day was:

😀 fantastic   🙂 good   😐 okay   🙁 not good   😟 awful

```
┌─────────────────────────────────────────┐
│ Teacher:                                │
│                                         │
└─────────────────────────────────────────┘
┌─────────────────────────────────────────┐
│ Parent:                                 │
│                                         │
└─────────────────────────────────────────┘
```

Tuesday

My day was:

😀 fantastic   🙂 good   😐 okay   🙁 not good   😟 awful

```
┌─────────────────────────────────────────┐
│ Teacher:                                │
│                                         │
└─────────────────────────────────────────┘
┌─────────────────────────────────────────┐
│ Parent:                                 │
│                                         │
└─────────────────────────────────────────┘
```

Wednesday

My day was:

😀 fantastic   🙂 good   😐 okay   🙁 not good   😟 awful

```
┌─────────────────────────────────────────┐
│ Teacher:                                │
│                                         │
└─────────────────────────────────────────┘
┌─────────────────────────────────────────┐
│ Parent:                                 │
│                                         │
└─────────────────────────────────────────┘
```

Thursday
My day was:

fantastic   good   okay   not good   awful

Teacher:

Parent:

Friday
My day was:

fantastic   good   okay   not good   awful

Teacher:

Parent:

Extra Space:

Monday   Week beginning: _____

My day was:

😄   🙂   😐   🙁   ☹️
fantastic   good   okay   not good   awful

┌───┐
│ Teacher: │
│   │
└───┘

┌───┐
│ Parent: │
│   │
└───┘

Tuesday

My day was:

😄   🙂   😐   🙁   ☹️
fantastic   good   okay   not good   awful

┌───┐
│ Teacher: │
│   │
└───┘

┌───┐
│ Parent: │
│   │
└───┘

Wednesday

My day was:

😄   🙂   😐   🙁   ☹️
fantastic   good   okay   not good   awful

┌───┐
│ Teacher: │
│   │
└───┘

┌───┐
│ Parent: │
│   │
└───┘

Thursday

My day was:

| fantastic | good | okay | not good | awful |

Teacher:

Parent:

Friday

My day was:

| fantastic | good | okay | not good | awful |

Teacher:

Parent:

Extra Space:

Monday   Week beginning: _____

My day was:

😄 fantastic   🙂 good   😐 okay   🙁 not good   ☹️ awful

Teacher:

Parent:

Tuesday

My day was:

😄 fantastic   🙂 good   😐 okay   🙁 not good   ☹️ awful

Teacher:

Parent:

Wednesday

My day was:

😄 fantastic   🙂 good   😐 okay   🙁 not good   ☹️ awful

Teacher:

Parent:

Thursday

My day was:

- fantastic
- good
- okay
- not good
- awful

Teacher:

Parent:

Friday

My day was:

- fantastic
- good
- okay
- not good
- awful

Teacher:

Parent:

Extra Space:

Monday   Week beginning: _____

My day was:

fantastic   good   okay   not good   awful

Teacher:

Parent:

Tuesday

My day was:

fantastic   good   okay   not good   awful

Teacher:

Parent:

Wednesday

My day was:

fantastic   good   okay   not good   awful

Teacher:

Parent:

Thursday

My day was:

- fantastic
- good
- okay
- not good
- awful

Teacher:

Parent:

Friday

My day was:

- fantastic
- good
- okay
- not good
- awful

Teacher:

Parent:

Extra Space:

Monday   Week beginning: _____

My day was:

😀 fantastic   🙂 good   😐 okay   🙁 not good   ☹️ awful

```
┌─────────────────────────────────────────────┐
│ Teacher:                                    │
│                                             │
└─────────────────────────────────────────────┘
```

```
┌─────────────────────────────────────────────┐
│ Parent:                                     │
│                                             │
└─────────────────────────────────────────────┘
```

Tuesday

My day was:

😀 fantastic   🙂 good   😐 okay   🙁 not good   ☹️ awful

```
┌─────────────────────────────────────────────┐
│ Teacher:                                    │
│                                             │
└─────────────────────────────────────────────┘
```

```
┌─────────────────────────────────────────────┐
│ Parent:                                     │
│                                             │
└─────────────────────────────────────────────┘
```

Wednesday

My day was:

😀 fantastic   🙂 good   😐 okay   🙁 not good   ☹️ awful

```
┌─────────────────────────────────────────────┐
│ Teacher:                                    │
│                                             │
└─────────────────────────────────────────────┘
```

```
┌─────────────────────────────────────────────┐
│ Parent:                                     │
│                                             │
└─────────────────────────────────────────────┘
```

Thursday

My day was:

- 😃 fantastic
- 🙂 good
- 😐 okay
- 🙁 not good
- ☹️ awful

Teacher:

Parent:

Friday

My day was:

- 😃 fantastic
- 🙂 good
- 😐 okay
- 🙁 not good
- ☹️ awful

Teacher:

Parent:

Extra Space:

Monday   Week beginning: _____

My day was:

fantastic   good   okay   not good   awful

Teacher:

Parent:

Tuesday

My day was:

fantastic   good   okay   not good   awful

Teacher:

Parent:

Wednesday

My day was:

fantastic   good   okay   not good   awful

Teacher:

Parent:

Thursday

My day was:

| fantastic | good | okay | not good | awful |

Teacher:

Parent:

Friday

My day was:

| fantastic | good | okay | not good | awful |

Teacher:

Parent:

Extra Space:

_____
_____
_____
_____
_____
_____
_____

Monday   **Week beginning:** _____

My day was:

fantastic   good   okay   not good   awful

Teacher:

Parent:

Tuesday

My day was:

fantastic   good   okay   not good   awful

Teacher:

Parent:

Wednesday

My day was:

fantastic   good   okay   not good   awful

Teacher:

Parent:

Thursday
My day was:

- 😄 fantastic
- 🙂 good
- 😐 okay
- 🙁 not good
- ☹️ awful

Teacher:

Parent:

Friday
My day was:

- 😄 fantastic
- 🙂 good
- 😐 okay
- 🙁 not good
- ☹️ awful

Teacher:

Parent:

Extra Space:

Monday Week beginning: _____

My day was:

| fantastic | good | okay | not good | awful |

Teacher:

Parent:

Tuesday

My day was:

| fantastic | good | okay | not good | awful |

Teacher:

Parent:

Wednesday

My day was:

| fantastic | good | okay | not good | awful |

Teacher:

Parent:

Thursday

My day was:

fantastic good okay not good awful

Teacher:

Parent:

Friday

My day was:

fantastic good okay not good awful

Teacher:

Parent:

Extra Space:

Monday   Week beginning: _____

My day was:

| fantastic | good | okay | not good | awful |

Teacher:

Parent:

Tuesday

My day was:

| fantastic | good | okay | not good | awful |

Teacher:

Parent:

Wednesday

My day was:

| fantastic | good | okay | not good | awful |

Teacher:

Parent:

Thursday

My day was:

| fantastic | good | okay | not good | awful |

Teacher:

Parent:

Friday

My day was:

| fantastic | good | okay | not good | awful |

Teacher:

Parent:

Extra Space:

Monday   Week beginning: _____

My day was:

fantastic   good   okay   not good   awful

Teacher:

Parent:

Tuesday

My day was:

fantastic   good   okay   not good   awful

Teacher:

Parent:

Wednesday

My day was:

fantastic   good   okay   not good   awful

Teacher:

Parent:

Thursday

My day was:

| fantastic | good | okay | not good | awful |

Teacher:

Parent:

Friday

My day was:

| fantastic | good | okay | not good | awful |

Teacher:

Parent:

Extra Space:

_____
_____
_____
_____
_____
_____
_____

www.ingramcontent.com/pod-product-compliance
Lightning Source LLC
Chambersburg PA
CBHW021449080526
44588CB00009B/763